Sharks
and other dangers of the deep!

Written by Simon Mugford
Designed by Matt Denny

priddy books
big ideas for little people

what is a shark?

They can sense prey with 'ampullae of Lorenzini' — electrical sensors under their skin

Excellent eyesight

Nostrils — sharks have a very good sense of smell

Mouth filled with lots of sharp teeth

Sharks take water in and pump it out through their gill slits

Sharks are a type of fish that have **existed** since before the **dinosaurs.** They can be **scary** and extremely **dangerous**, but a shark is one of the most **incredible** creatures on Earth.

There are more than **300** different **types** of sharks, and they are found in oceans all over the world. They come in many **shapes** and sizes, from the **size** of your arm to some that are **bigger** than a bus!

First dorsal fin

Second dorsal fin

Caudal fin

Anal fin

Pelvic fin

'Lateral line' of nerves to sense movements

Pectoral fin

Each shark and creature in this book has been given a 'danger rating' from zero jaws to five:

Harmless

Harmful, unlikely to attack

Very harmful, unlikely to attack

Likely to attack and hurt

Very dangerous — will hurt very badly

Deadly — very likely to attack and kill!

To help you imagine how big they are, you can compare their sizes to an adult.

The great white is most people's idea of a 'killer shark'. They are large, fearsome predators, and although they have attacked people, a great white would much rather eat a seal or sea lion! This shark's teeth are razor-sharp, jagged, and arranged in rows. Like in all sharks, when a tooth breaks off, another one moves into its place.

Skin covered in 'denticles' — very rough, sharp scales

Average length: **14 ft (4.2 m)**

Danger rating

Great white shark

The great white can have as many as 3,000 teeth at one time

Large black eyes, with very good eyesight

The biggest great white on record was 23 feet (7 m) long

There are few scarier sights than a shark's dorsal fin on the water surface

Scarred skin, caused by unfortunate prey fighting back

Hammerhead shark

Having eyes in this position allows the shark to 'scan' large areas for prey

The shape of its head helps the hammerhead steer itself in the water

The hammerhead's teeth are relatively small, but they are very jagged and sharp

This shark has an **unusually** wide, hammer-shaped head. Its **eyes** are on each side of its head and its first **dorsal** fin is very large and pointed. This weird-looking **shark** has very good **senses** for finding prey.

Average length: 11 ft (3.3 m)

Danger rating

These sharks live in the coastal parts of warm, tropical oceans

Tiger shark

Tiger sharks have been found with cans, bottles and other garbage in their stomachs!

Tiger **sharks** get their name from the striped **markings** along their sides. They will **eat** almost anything, and given the chance, will **attack** any people nearby.

Average length: 10 ft (3 m)

Danger rating

Whale shark

Whale sharks can live to be 150 years old

Huge mouth, up to 4 feet (1.2 m) wide

Average length: 26 ft (8 m)

Danger rating

Every whale shark has a unique pattern of spots

On its tail, the top fin is much larger than the lower fin

Whale sharks use their entire bodies to swim, not just their fins

The magnificent whale shark is the largest shark (and the largest fish) in the world. It uses its very large mouth to filter plankton out of the sea to eat. It is a slow-moving, gentle giant and is harmless to people. Whale sharks have distinctive spotted and striped markings all over their very rough and thick skin.

This shark, also called the **ragged-tooth** shark, is not actually as scary as it looks. Sand tigers spend most of their time slowly **swimming** around reefs and wrecks, feeding on **squid** and slippery fish, which their teeth are **designed** to catch.

Average length: 10 ft (3 m)

Danger rating

Sand tigers gulp air and then burp to control their buoyancy!

Sand tiger shark

Blue shark

This beautiful,
fast-swimming shark
is prized by fishermen
around the world

This shark is also
known as the blue dog,
or blue whaler shark

Blue sharks are found in the deep
waters of oceans all over the world, where they
often form large groups, or 'schools' of sharks.
They are long and sleek with a pointed snout, and
are fast swimmers. Their name comes from the
distinctive purple-blue color of their skin.

Average length: 12 ft (3.6 m)

Danger rating

Basking sharks are **huge,** but have very tiny, almost **useless** teeth. Like the whale shark, it filters its **food** out of the water using gill rakers. Also called **sunfish,** they spend most of their time close to the water surface, **'basking'** in the sun.

Very rough skin

'Gill rakers' filter food from the water

Average length: 23 ft (7 m)

Danger rating

Basking shark

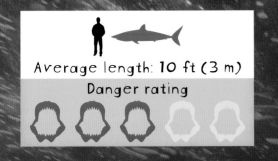

Average length: 10 ft (3 m)

Danger rating

Of all sharks, makos are the **fastest** swimmers. They can reach speeds of up to 20 mph (32 km/h) and leap high out of the water. Fishermen like to catch makos, but are often bitten when they reel them in!

Large, black eyes

Razor-sharp teeth are long and smooth

Mako shark

Wobbegong shark

Average length: 6 ft (1.8 m)

Danger rating

Spotted pattern skin

Long, flat and flexible body

The wobbegong shark's **unusual** markings help to keep them **hidden** in the coral reefs in which they live. Wobbegongs are **nocturnal,** and rest on the sea bottom in the day. They are not aggressive, but if **disturbed** they will give a very **nasty** bite and will not let go!

Nurse shark

Average length: 6 ft (1.8 m)

Danger rating

Unlike most sharks, their skin is smooth

Nurse sharks use whisker-like organs called 'barbels' to touch and taste for food on the sea bottom

These **slow-moving** sharks feed on **shellfish** on the sea bottom, where they use their strong pectoral fins to 'walk' through the sand. Nurse sharks will not **attack** unless they are **disturbed**, but have a very powerful, crushing bite.

Reef shark

This blacktip reef shark is one of the most common sharks in the world. It lives around coral reefs in the Indian and Pacific Oceans. It is fairly harmless, but has been known to bite people wading in shallow water.

ke most
are
lig ath
and

Black tips at the ends of its fins

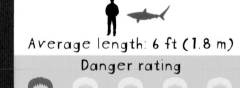

Average length: 6 ft (1.8 m)

Danger rating

The **bull** shark is the type of shark that **attacks** people most often. This is mainly because it **lives** in shallow, coastal areas. They are the only sharks that can live in **freshwater** and have been found many miles **inland** up the Amazon River in South America.

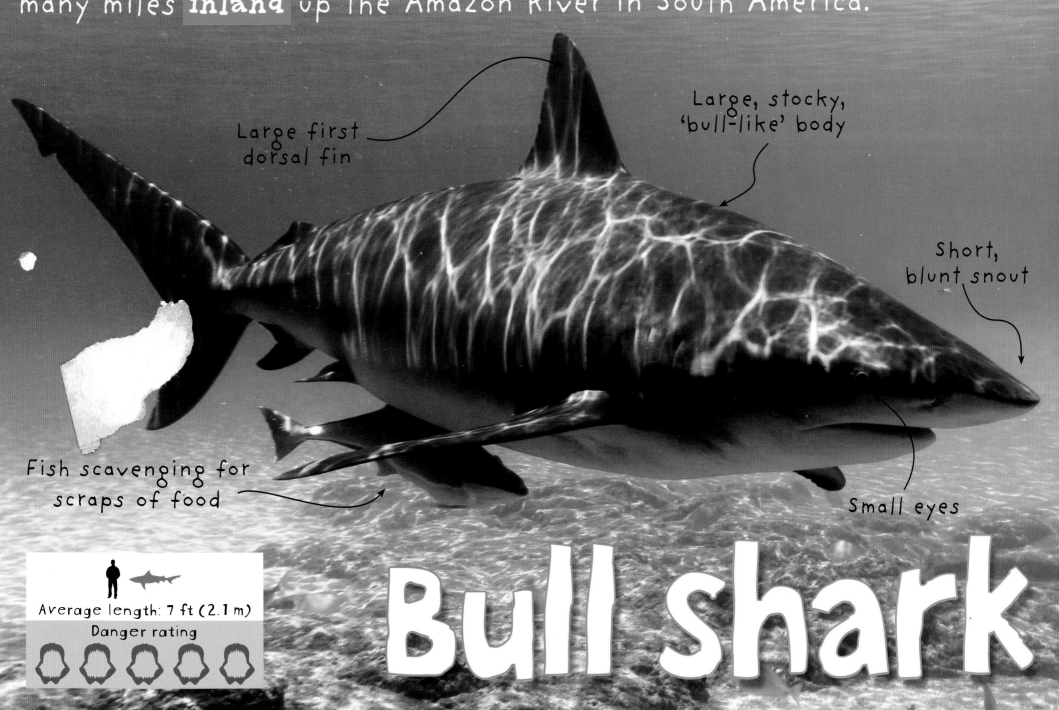

Large first dorsal fin

Large, stocky, 'bull-like' body

Short, blunt snout

Fish scavenging for scraps of food

Small eyes

Average length: 7 ft (2.1 m)

Danger rating

Bull shark

white tip shark

Very large,
white-tipped
dorsal fin

Stocky,
powerful
body

White tips are
known to follow
pilot whales,
looking for food

Average length: 10 ft (3 m)

Danger rating

Large **groups** of oceanic white tips have been
known to attack people **stranded** in the water
after **shipwrecks** and air crashes. They are **deep-sea**
sharks and are thought to **migrate** over long distances.

Fins used to funnel food into its mouth

Huge pectoral fins or 'wings'

Long tail

Gill slits

Rays are closely related to **sharks**. The giant manta ray is the **largest** type and can grow to 30 feet (9 m) wide. It is **harmless** to people, but a blow from one of its **'wings'** would certainly pack a **fearsome** punch!

Average width: 22 ft (6.7 m)
Danger rating

Manta ray

These rays live in the warm, **tropical** parts of the Atlantic Ocean and Caribbean, where they **feed** almost constantly. They have poisonous **spines** in their tails which they use to defend themselves against **predators** — mainly sharks!

Stinging spine in tail

A stingray's tail can be twice as long as its body

Eyes on top of head

Stingray

Average width: 3 ft (1 m)

Danger rating

Eagle ray

Eagle rays sometimes travel in large schools, 'flying' at the surface

Pointed snout

Mouth

These very large, beautiful spotted rays can grow up to around 15 feet (4.5 m) long. They are very powerful swimmers and are able to jump several feet above the surface of the water.

Electric ray

Electric rays lie in wait for their **prey** or hover silently over them, before stunning them with a powerful **electric** shock. These creatures have little to fear from predators, and they will **chase** after divers!

Electric organs in the ray's center can deliver the shock up or down

Tail and fin

This ray is also known as a 'numbfish'

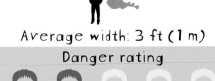

Average width: 3 ft (1 m)

Danger rating

Green moray

This long, snake-like fish gets its name from the green slime that covers its body. It spends most of the time hidden inside rocks with only its head poking out. A large green moray can give a very nasty, potentially lethal bite.

Average length: 6 ft (1.8 m)

Danger rating

These **tropical** fish live and feed around shallow **coral** reefs in Asia. They are very **colorful** and pretty, but touching their spines releases a **powerful** venom — the lionfish is one of the most poisonous fish in the world.

Poisonous spines

Lionfish

Average length: 12 in (30 cm)

Danger rating

Jellyfish

Average length: 3 ft (1 m)

Danger rating

This part of the jellyfish is called the 'hood'

Jellyfish often travel in huge groups

Stinging tentacles

Jellyfish **float** in the sea and drift along with ocean tides and currents, feeding on **plankton** as they move. The tentacles of jellyfish release a type of **sting** or poison. Few people survive a sting from a box jellyfish, which is the most **poisonous** creature on Earth.

This unusual tropical fish has an excellent way of **defending** itself against predators. When it is **threatened,** it gulps water into its **mouth** and inflates itself into a **spiked** poisonous ball!

Tiny mouth

Sharp spikes

Length: 12 in (30 cm)
Danger rating

Porcupinefish

Blue-ringed octopus

Eye

Suction pads

Tentacle

Blue rings

This is the **smallest** octopus in the world, but it is also the most **deadly**. The blue rings only appear when the octopus is alarmed. Its venom is fatal, and it carries enough to kill 26 adult humans within a few minutes.

Average length: 15 in (38 cm)

Danger rating

Glossary

Ampullae of Lorenzini Sensors beneath a shark's skin that pick up tiny amounts of electricity given off by animals.

Anal fin Small fin on the underside of a shark's body, close to its tail.

Barbels Whisker-like feelers beneath some sharks' mouths that help them touch and taste.

Buoyancy The ability to float. Sharks have to keep moving to remain buoyant.

Caudal fin The shark's tail — used to move forward through the water.

Coral reef Coral are living creatures with a hard outer skeleton. When they group together, they form a coral reef, which attracts lots of sea life, including sharks and rays.

Denticles Small, very hard tooth-like scales that cover a shark's body.

Dorsal fin Fin on a shark's back that keeps it stable as it swims. There are usually two — the larger, first dorsal fin, and a smaller second one.

Gill rakers Large organs inside the mouths of whale and basking sharks that filter out plankton from the water.

Gill slits The openings that allow water to pass over a shark's gills.